# THE LETTER A

Trace the letter A:
Write an upper and lower case letter A:
Color all the items that begin with the letter A:

# THE LETTER B

Trace the letter B:

Write an upper and lower case letter B:

Color all the items that begin with the letter B:

# THE LETTER C

Trace the letter C:

Write an upper and lower case letter C:

Color all the items that begin with the letter C:

# THE LETTER D

Trace the letter D:

Write an upper and lower case letter D:

Color all the items that begin with the letter D:

# THE LETTER E

Trace the letter E:

Write an upper and lower case letter E:

Color all the items that begin with the letter E:

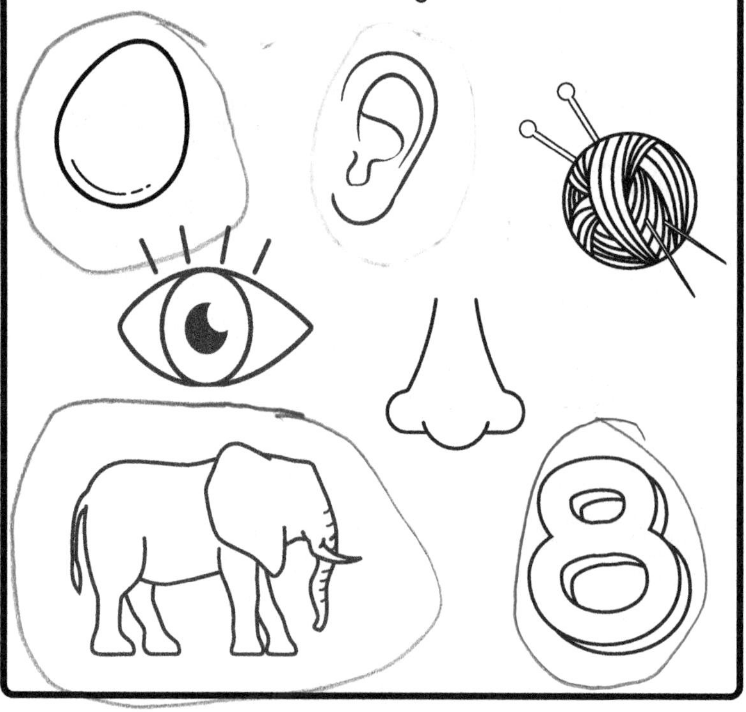

# THE LETTER F

Trace the letter F:

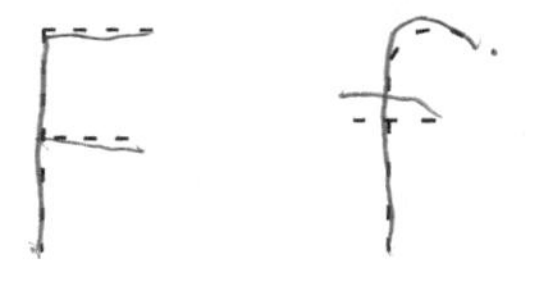

Write an upper and lower case letter F:

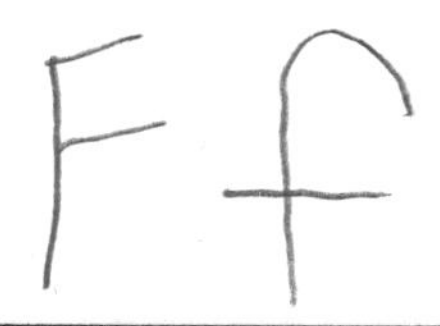

Color all the items that begin with the letter F:

# THE LETTER G

Trace the letter G:

Write an upper and lower case letter G:

Color all the items that begin with the letter G:

THE LETTER H
Trace the letter H:
Write an upper and lower case letter H:
Color all the items that begin with the letter H:

Trace the letter I:

Write an upper and lower case letter I:

Color all the items that begin with the letter I:

Trace the letter J:

Write an upper and lower case letter J:

Color all the items that begin with the letter J:

# THE LETTER K

Trace the letter K:

Write an upper and lower case letter K:

Color all the items that begin with the letter K:

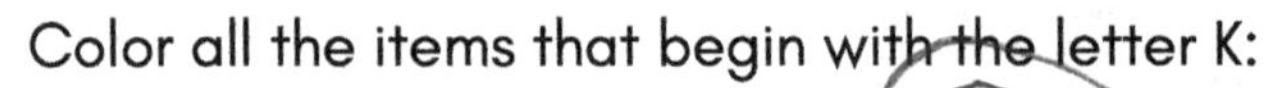

# THE LETTER L

Trace the letter L:

Write an upper and lower case letter L:

Color all the items that begin with the letter L:

# THE LETTER M

Trace the letter M:

Write an upper and lower case letter M:

Color all the items that begin with the letter M:

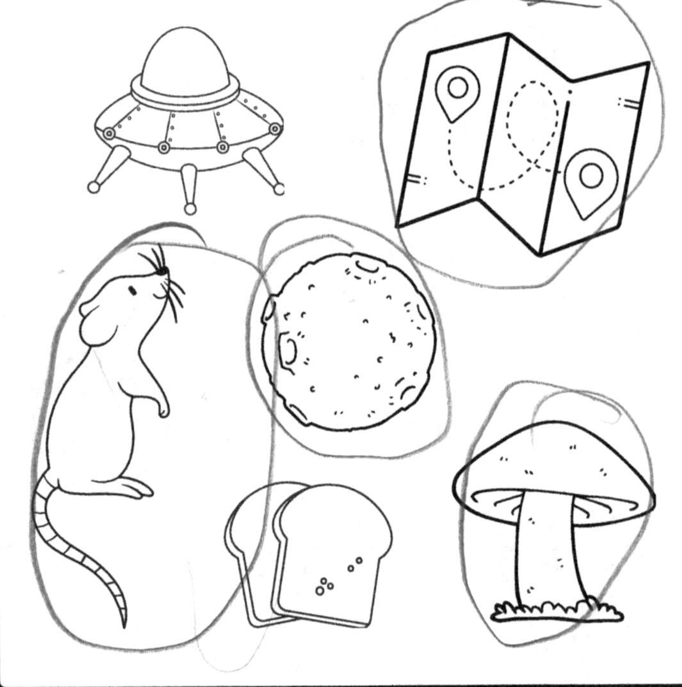

# THE LETTER N

Trace the letter N:

N n

Write an upper and lower case letter N:

Color all the items that begin with the letter N:

# THE LETTER O

Trace the letter O:

Write an upper and lower case letter O:

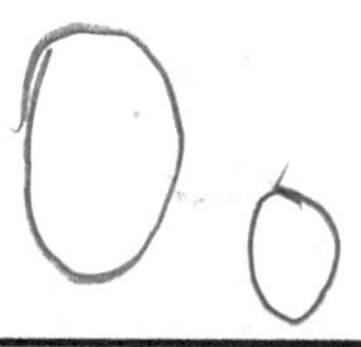

Color all the items that begin with the letter O:

# THE LETTER P

Trace the letter P:

Write an upper and lower case letter P:

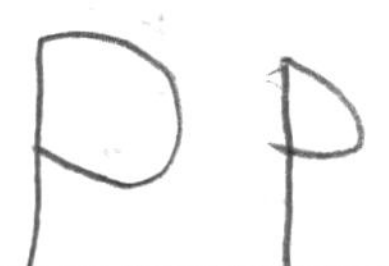

Color all the items that begin with the letter P:

# THE LETTER Q

Trace the letter Q:

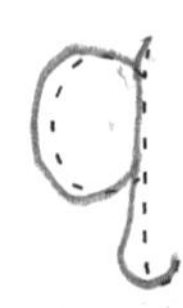

Write an upper and lower case letter Q:

Color all the items that begin with the letter Q:

Trace the letter R:

Write an upper and lower case letter R:

Color all the items that begin with the letter R:

# THE LETTER S

Trace the letter S:

Write an upper and lower case letter S:

Color all the items that begin with the letter S:

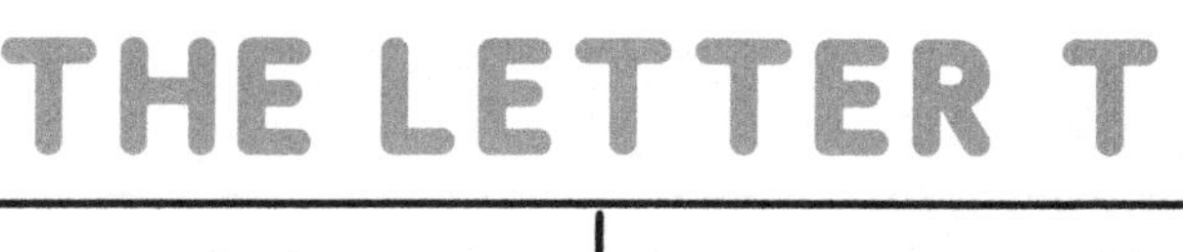


Trace the letter T:

Write an upper and lower case letter T:

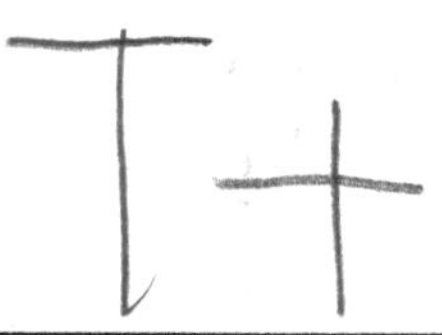

Color all the items that begin with the letter T:

Trace the letter U:

Write an upper and lower case letter U:

Color all the items that begin with the letter U:

# THE LETTER V

Trace the letter V:

Write an upper and lower case letter V:

Color all the items that begin with the letter V:

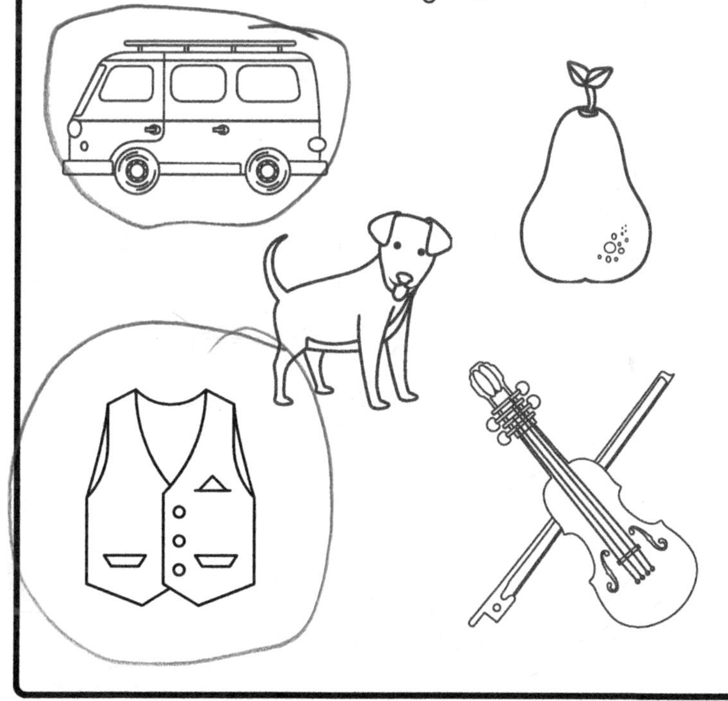

# THE LETTER W

Trace the letter W

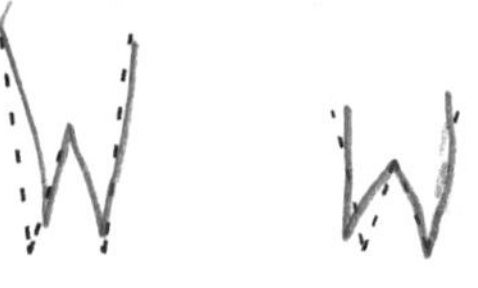

Write an upper and lower case letter W:

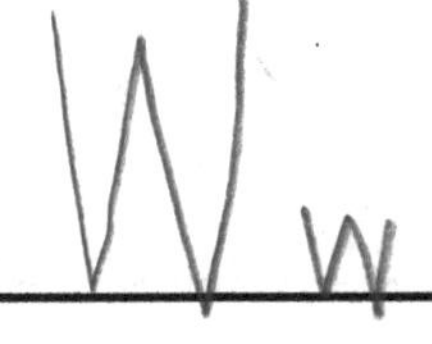

Color all the items that begin with the letter W:

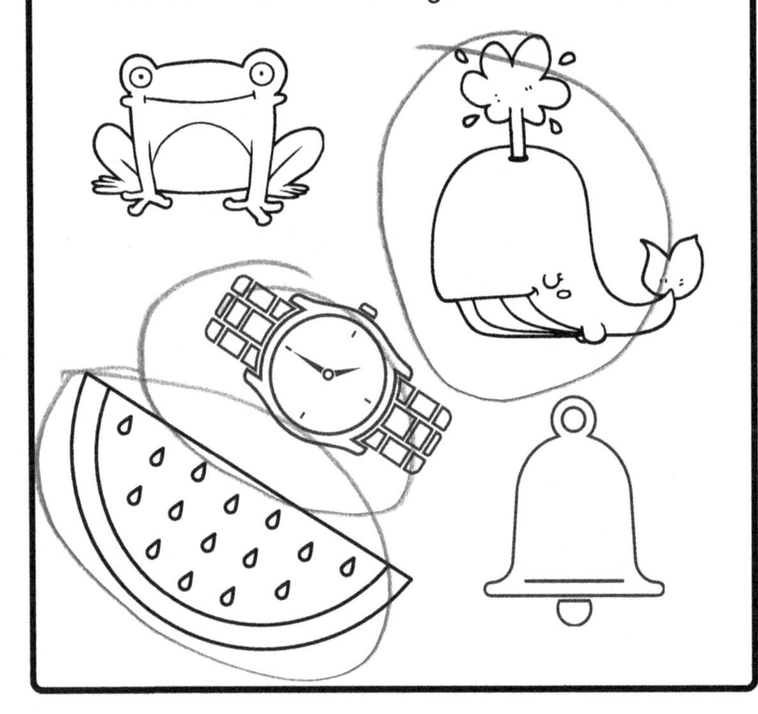

# THE LETTER X

Trace the letter X

Write an upper and lower case letter X:

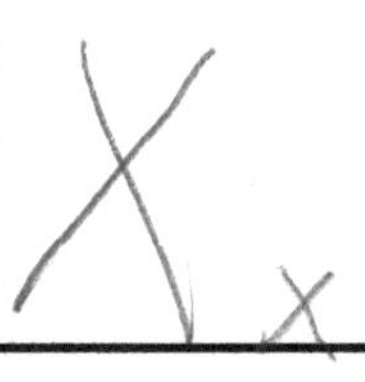

Color all the items that begin with the letter X:

Trace the letter Y

Write an upper and lower case letter Y:

Color all the items that begin with the letter Y:

# THE LETTER Z

Trace the letter Z

Z z

Write an upper and lower case letter Z:

Color all the items that begin with the letter Z:

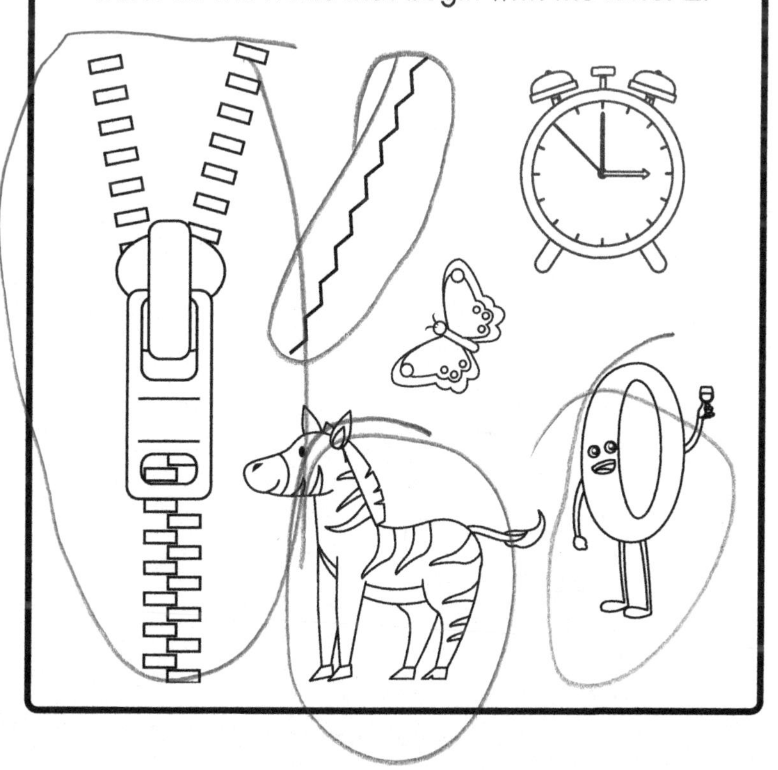

# Aa

A

a

A

a

# Bb

B

b

B

b

# Cc

C

c

C

c

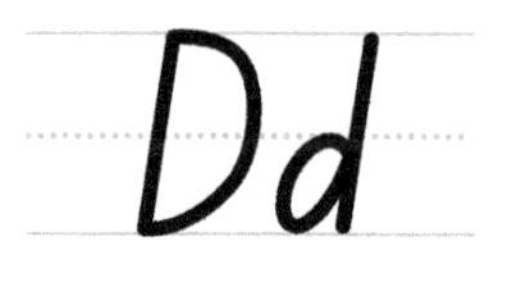

Dingo

Practise your uppercase and lowercase Ds below:

Trace these words that begin with the letter D:

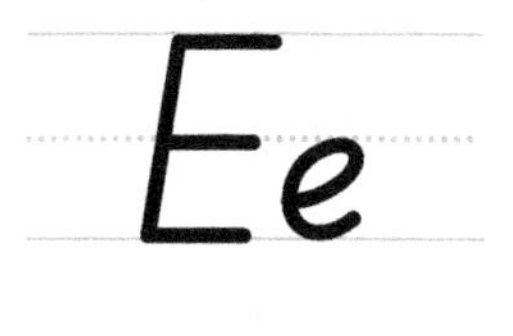

Echidna

Practise your uppercase and lowercase Es below:

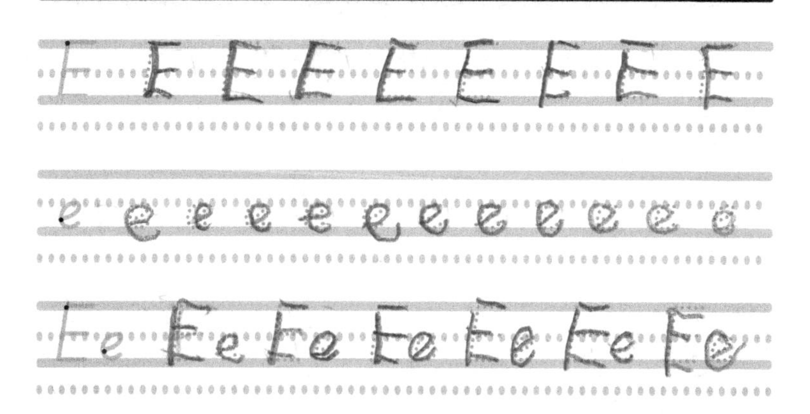

Trace these words that begin with the letter E:

Frog

Practise your uppercase and lowercase Fs below:

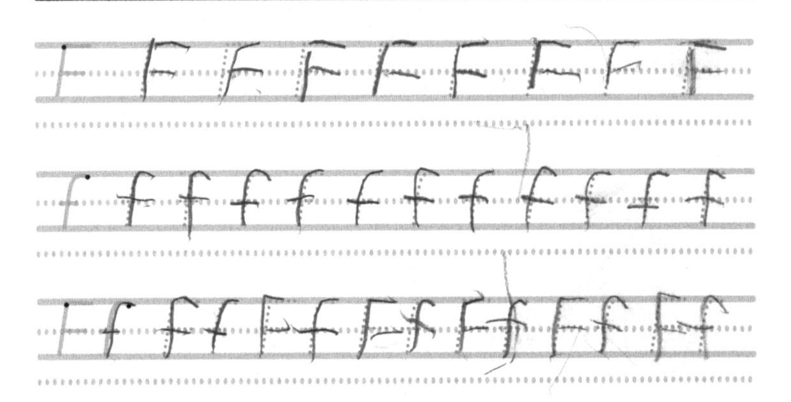

Trace these words that begin with the letter F:

Gg

Practise your uppercase and lowercase Gs below:

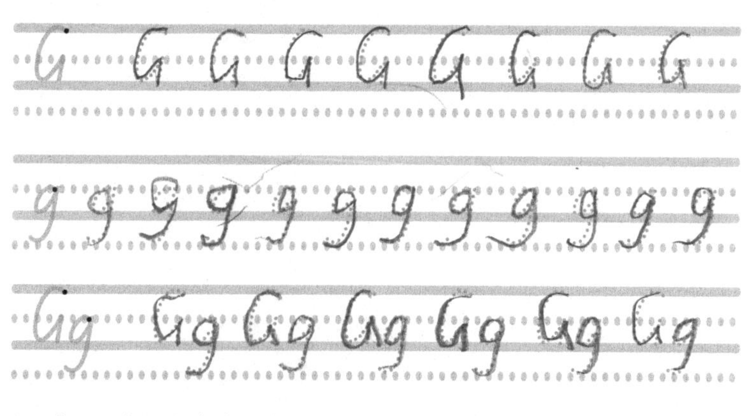

Trace these words that begin with the letter G:

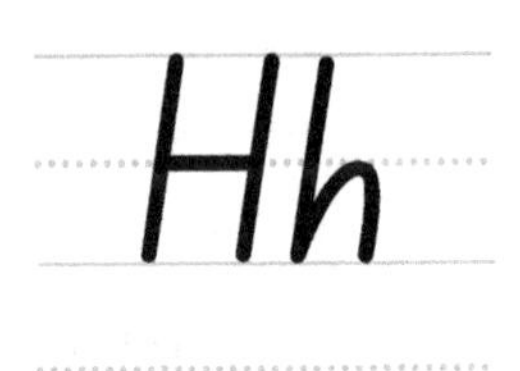

Huntsman Spider

Practise your uppercase and lowercase Hs below:

H H H H H H H H H

h h h h h h h h h h h h

Hh Hh Hh Hh Hh Hh Hh

Trace these words that begin with the letter H:

Hat

Hand

Horse

Hammer

Practise your uppercase and lowercase Is below:

I I I I I I I I I I I

i i i i i i i i i i i i i

Ii Ii Ii Ii Ii Ii Ii Ii Ii

Trace these words that begin with the letter I:

Ink

Iron

Island

Ice cream

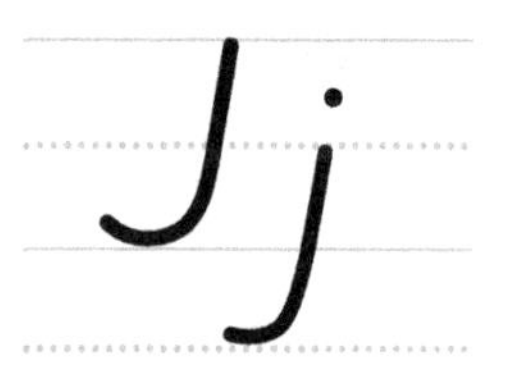

Practise your uppercase and lowercase Js below:

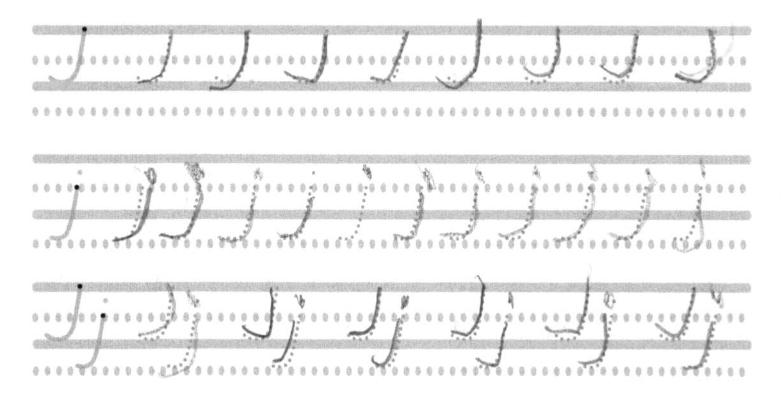

Trace these words that begin with the letter J:

# Kk

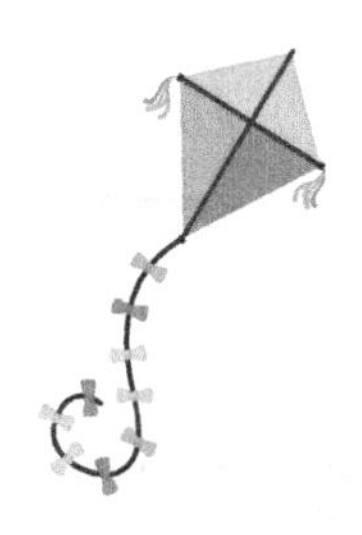

K

k

K

k

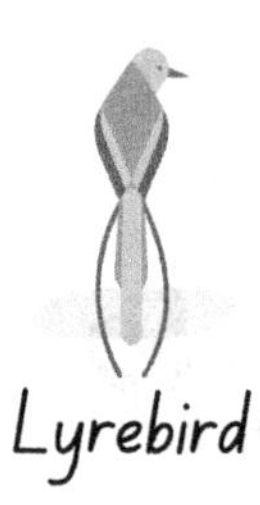

Lyrebird

Practise your uppercase and lowercase Ls below:

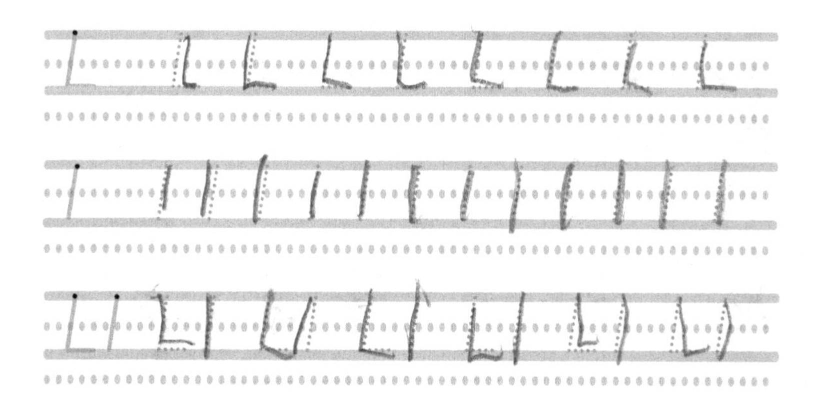

Trace these words that begin with the letter L:

# Mm

M

m

M

m

# Nn

N N N N N N

n n n n n n

N

n

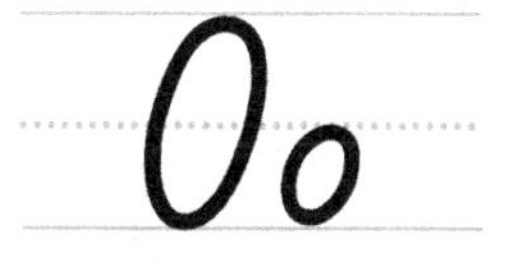

Oo

Orca

Practise your uppercase and lowercase Os below:

O O O O O O O O O

o o o o o o o o o o o o

Oo Oo Oo Oo Oo Oo Oo

Trace these words that begin with the letter O:

Owl

Oboe

Orange

Octopus

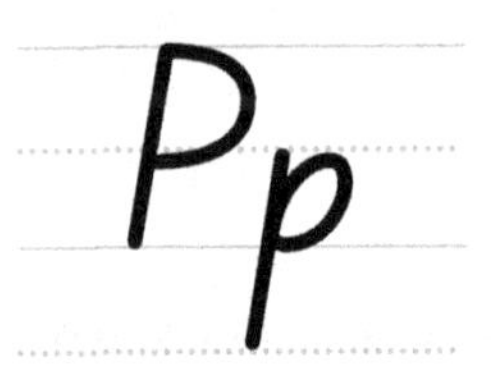

Platypus

Practise your uppercase and lowercase Ps below:

Trace these words that begin with the letter P:

Peg

Pear

Pencil

Penguin

Qq

Quokka

Practise your uppercase and lowercase Qs below:

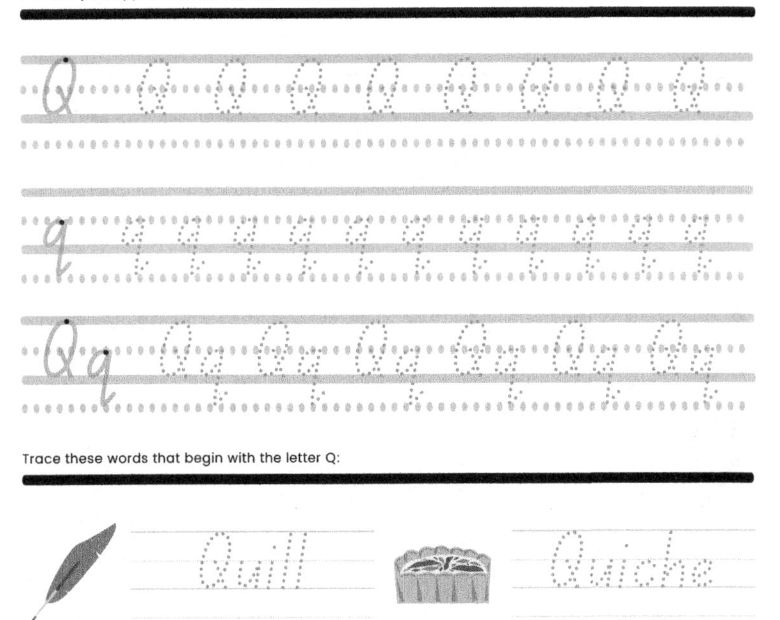

Trace these words that begin with the letter Q:

Quill

Quiche

Quarter

Question

Made in Canva

# Rr

R R R R R R

r r r r r r

R

r

# Ss

S S S S S S

s s s s s s

S

s

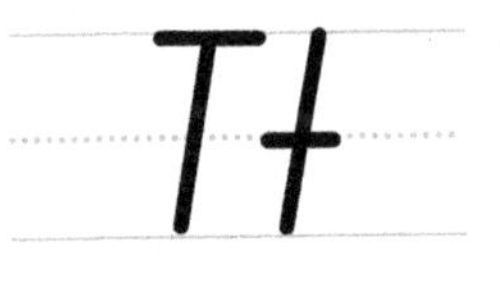

Practise your uppercase and lowercase Ts below:

Trace these words that begin with the letter T:

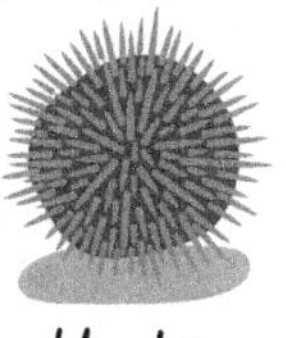

Urchin

Practise your uppercase and lowercase Us below:

U U U U U U U U U

u u u u u u u u u u u u u

Uu Uu Uu Uu Uu Uu Uu

Trace these words that begin with the letter U:

UFO

Uncle

Unicorn

Umbrella

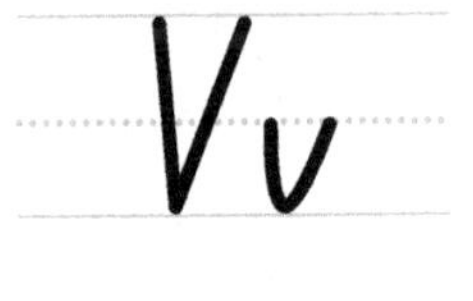

Velvet Gecko

Practise your uppercase and lowercase Vs below:

Trace these words that begin with the letter V:

Van

Vote

Violin

Vacuum

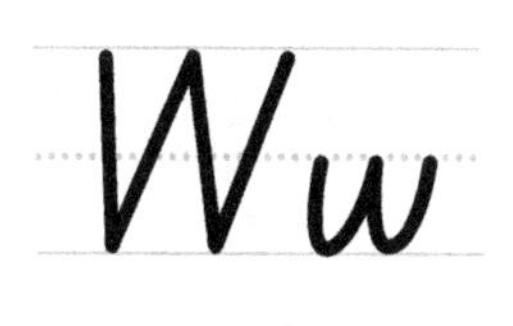

Wombat

Practise your uppercase and lowercase Ws below:

W W W W W W W W

w w w w w w w w w w w

Ww Ww Ww Ww Ww Ww

Trace these words that begin with the letter W:

Web

Wash

Whale

Window

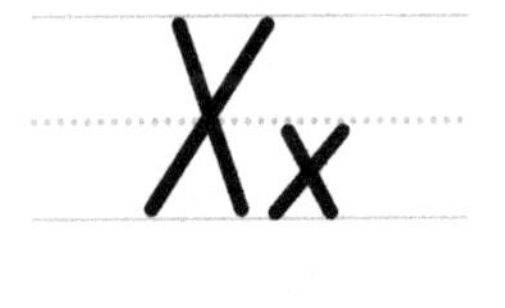

Xenicus
(New Zealand Wren)

Practise your uppercase and lowercase Xs below:

Trace these words that begin with the letter X:

X-ray Xiphias

Ximenia Xylophone

# Yy

Y Y Y Y Y Y

y y y y y y

Y

y

# Zz

Zebra Finch

Practise your uppercase and lowercase Zs below:

Trace these words that begin with the letter Z:

Zoo

Zebra

Zipper

Zucchini

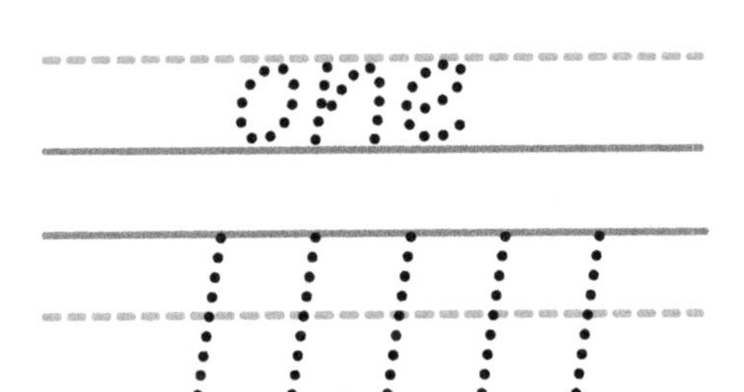

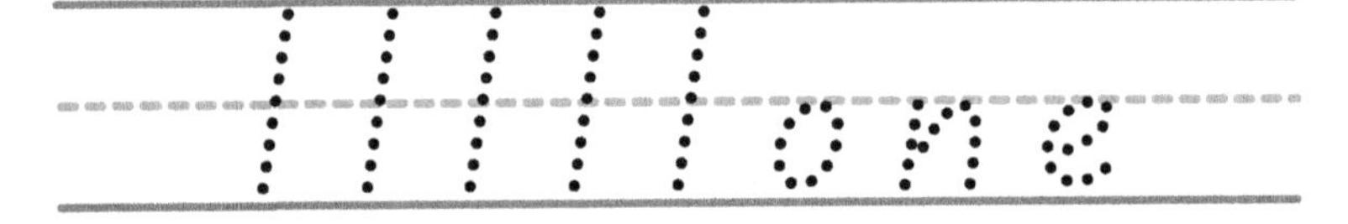

COLOR ONE STAR:

CIRCLE THE ONES:

1 3 5

4 2 1

6 1 8

1 7 1

2 1 4

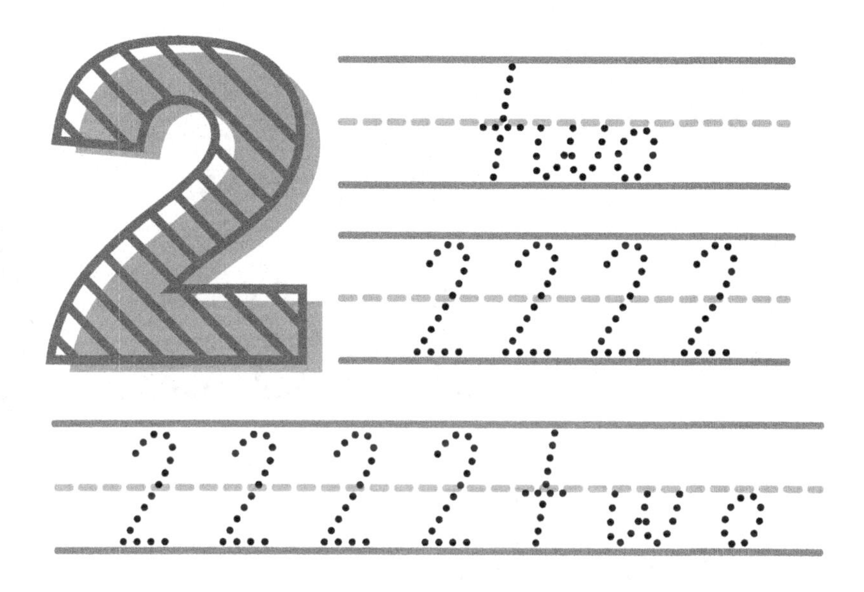


COLOR TWO TRIANGLES:

CIRCLE THE TWOS:

| | | |
|---|---|---|
| 2 | 3 | 5 |
| 4 | 2 | 1 |
| 6 | 1 | 2 |
| 1 | 2 | 1 |
| 2 | 1 | 4 |

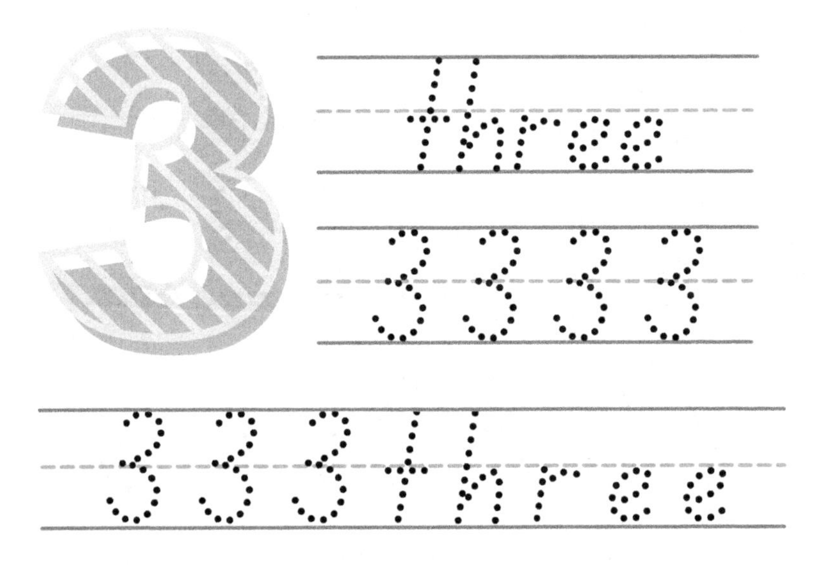


COLOR THREE SQUARES:

CIRCLE THE THREES:

| | | |
|---|---|---|
| 2 | 3 | 5 |
| 4 | 2 | 3 |
| 3 | 1 | 2 |
| 3 | 5 | 1 |
| 6 | 3 | 4 |

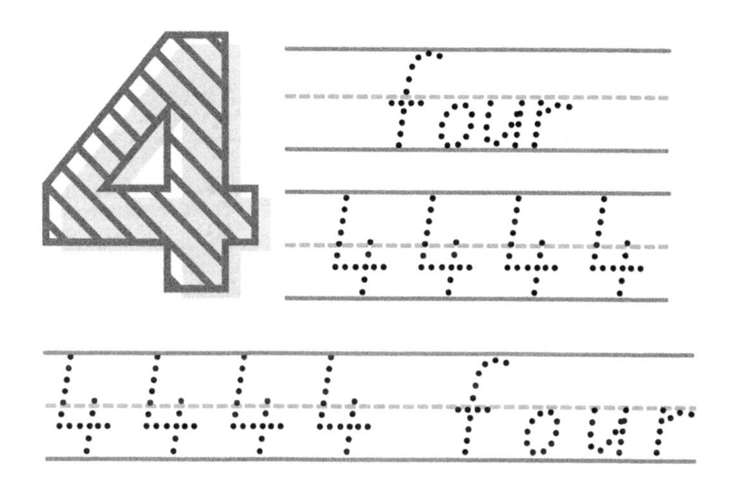

CIRCLE THE FOURS:

1 2 3

4 5 4

3 1 2

4 3 5

2 1 4

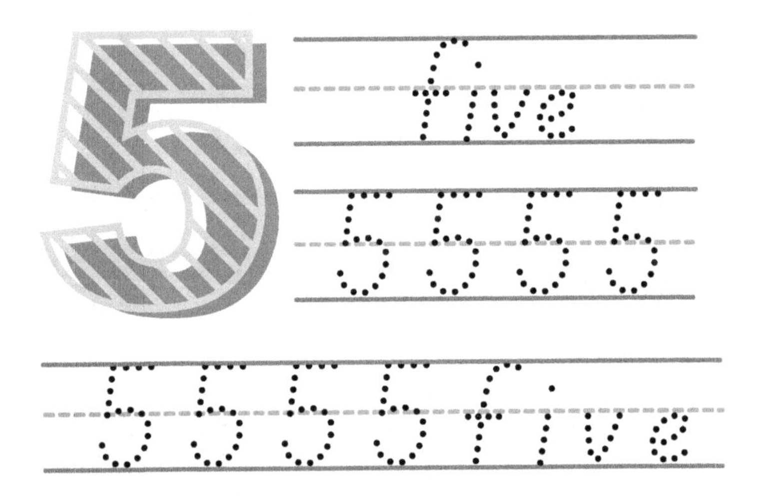


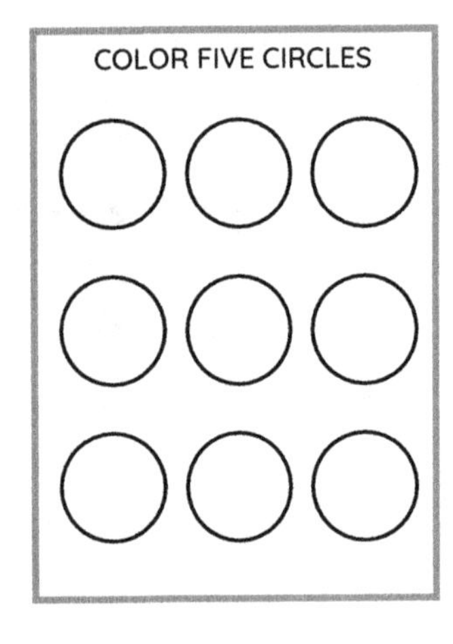


CIRCLE THE FIVES

5 2 3

1 5 4

3 5 2

4 3 5

2 5 4

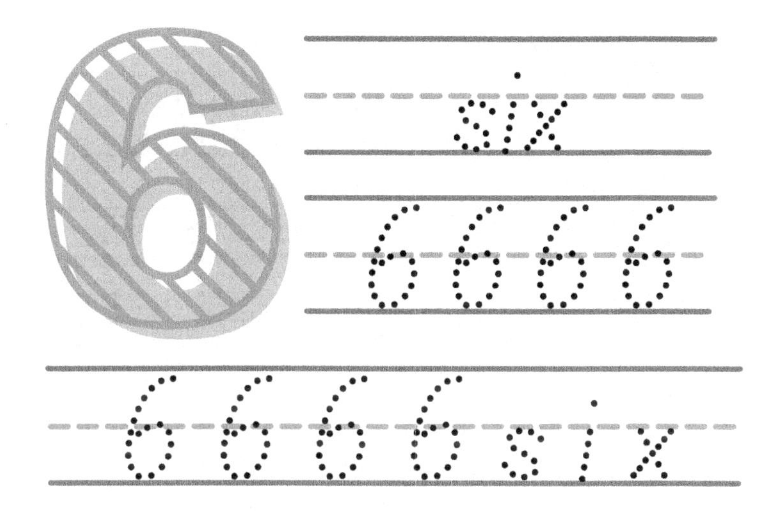


COLOR SIX TRIANGLES:

△ △ △

△ △ △

△ △ △

CIRCLE THE SIXES

| | | |
|---|---|---|
| 5 | 6 | 3 |
| 1 | 2 | 6 |
| 6 | 5 | 4 |
| 4 | 3 | 6 |
| 2 | 6 | 1 |

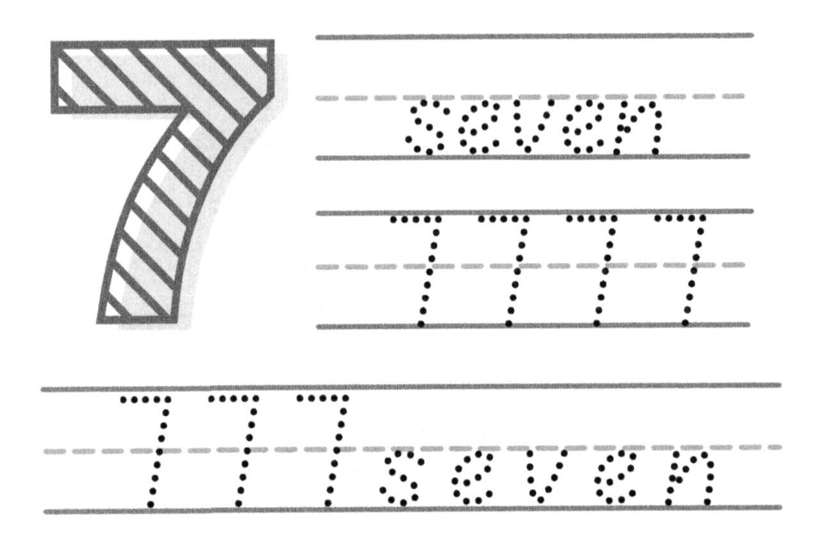


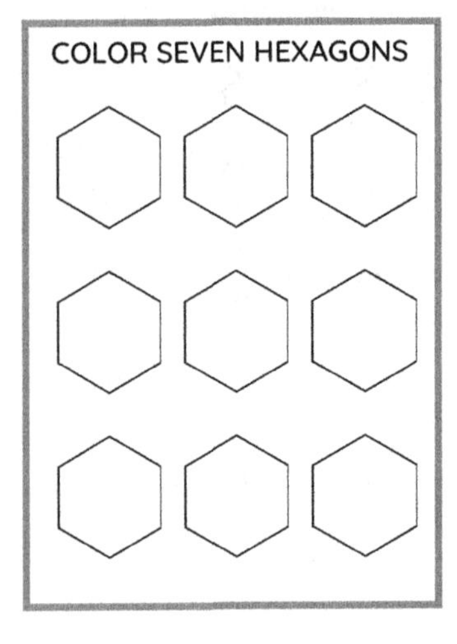


CIRCLE THE SEVENS

| | | |
|---|---|---|
| 5 | 7 | 3 |
| 1 | 7 | 4 |
| 7 | 3 | 2 |
| 4 | 2 | 7 |
| 7 | 5 | 4 |

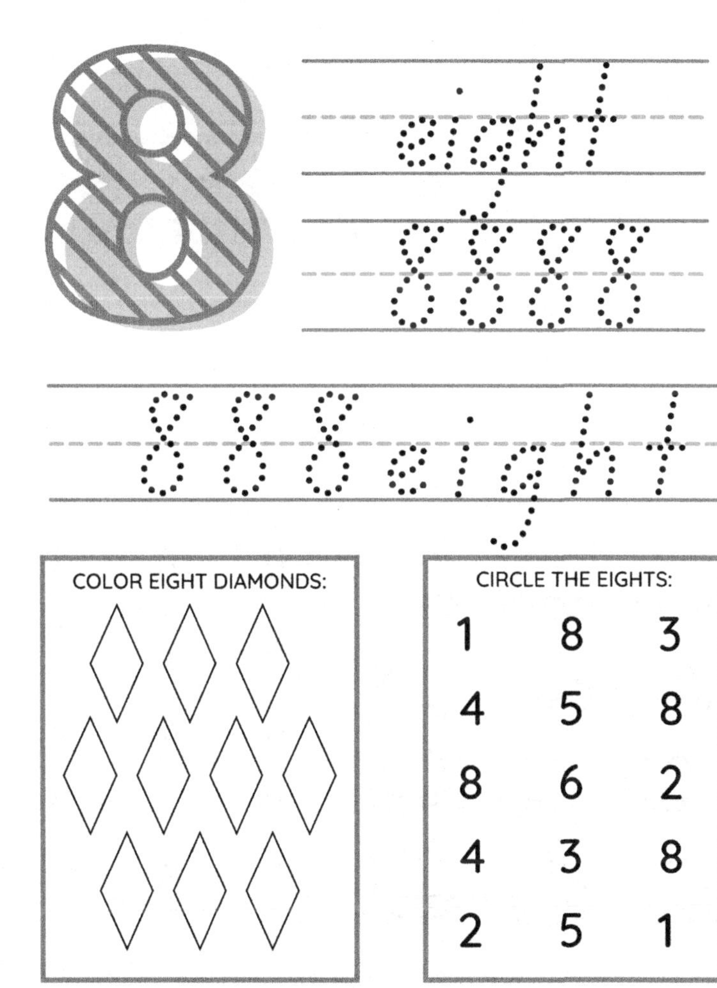
eight
8 8 8 8
8 8 8 eight
COLOR EIGHT DIAMONDS:
CIRCLE THE EIGHTS:
1 8 3
4 5 8
8 6 2
4 3 8
2 5 1

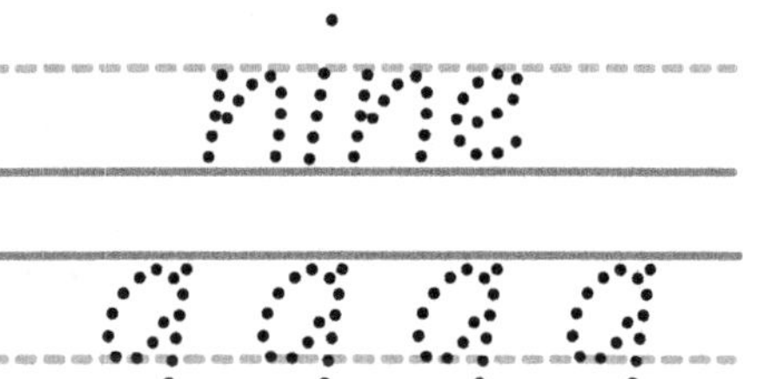


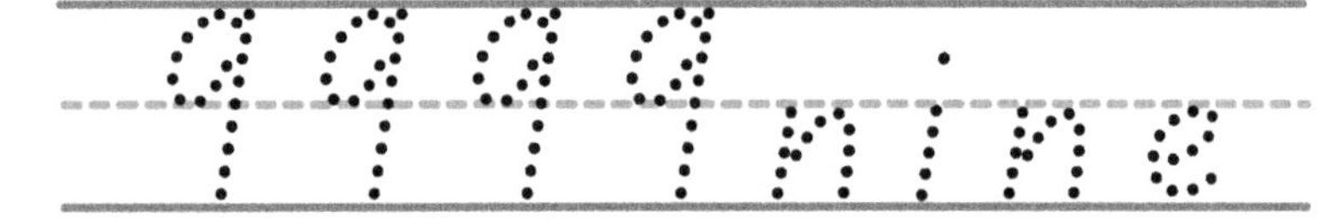

CIRCLE THE NINES:

| | | |
|---|---|---|
| 9 | 8 | 6 |
| 4 | 7 | 9 |
| 8 | 6 | 9 |
| 4 | 9 | 8 |
| 9 | 5 | 1 |

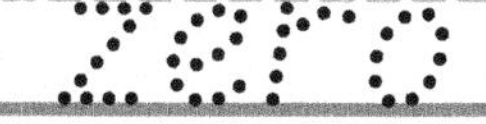

0 0 0 zero

COLOR ZERO OVALS:

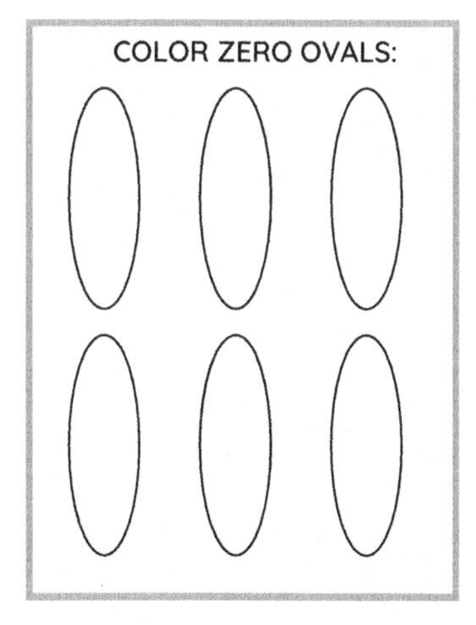

CIRCLE THE ZEROES:

| | | |
|---|---|---|
| 5 | 0 | 3 |
| 1 | 0 | 2 |
| 0 | 5 | 4 |
| 4 | 0 | 6 |
| 0 | 6 | 1 |

# ABC LOWERCASE APPLES

Practice your lowercase letter writing in the apples below. When finished color the apples that contain vowels using the color green.

# ABC UPPERCASE APPLES

Practice your uppercase letter writing in the apples below. When finished color the apples that contain vowels.

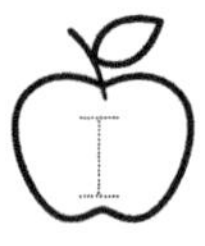

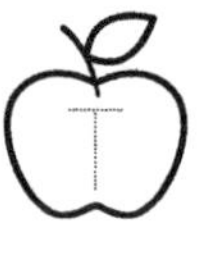

## CAR NUMBERS

Trace the numbers showing in the cars below. When finished, color the cars.

## NUMBERS OR LETTERS

Directions: Trace the numbers and letters. Color the raindrops with letters blue. Color the raindrops with numbers green.

# Number Practice 1-20

**PRACTICE COUNTING. FILL IN THE BLANKS WITH THE MISSING NUMBERS.**

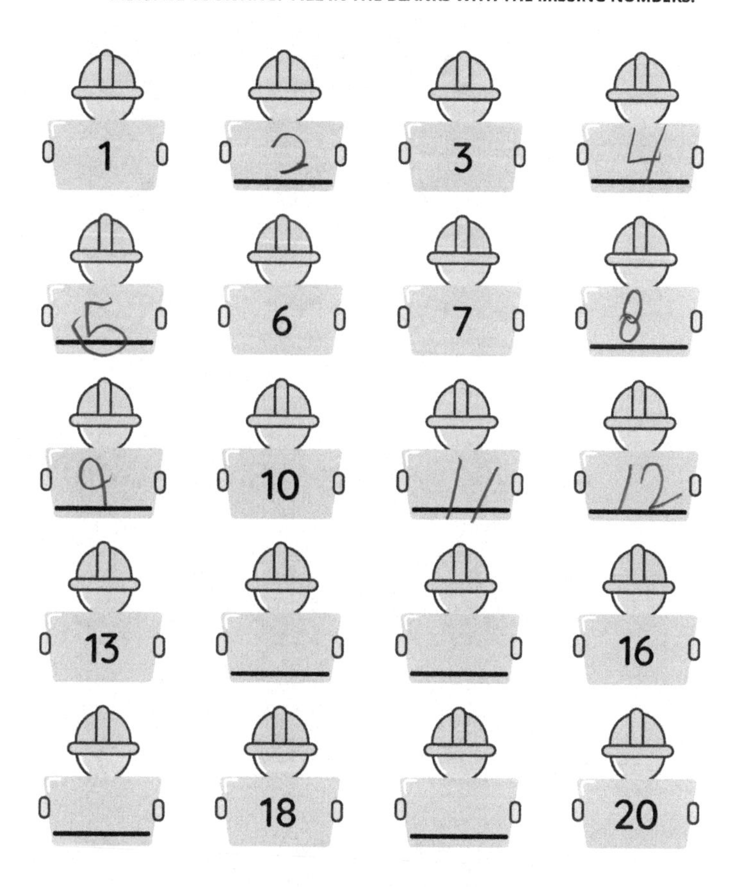

# Count & Color

Count and color the exact number of ocean animals

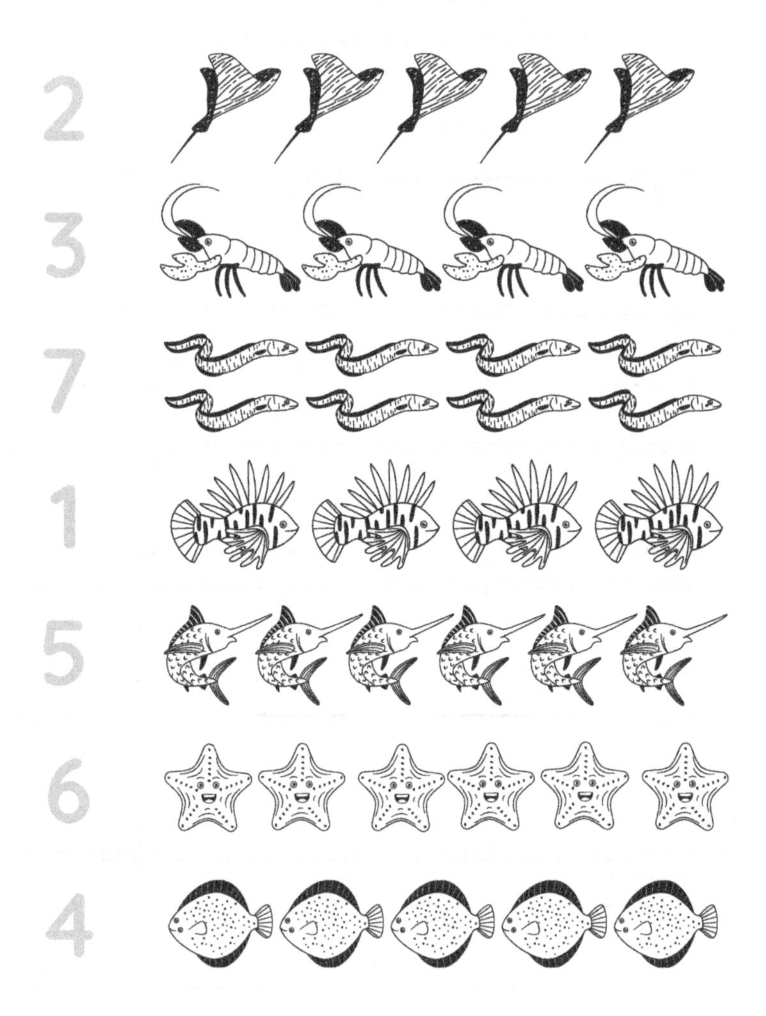

Made in the USA
Middletown, DE
21 July 2021

44552518R00046